Quick Instant Pot Cookbook

Simple Delicious **5-Ingredient or Less** Instant Pot Pressure Cooker Recipes to Save Time and Money, **Anyone Can Cook Effortlessly**

By Coco Randolph

Table of Contents

PREFACE

Greetings! Welcome to the Quick Instant Pot Cooking world!

If you are a busy person who wants to enjoy some authentic home cooked meals, but feel the hesitation to get into the complex process of cooking, then the instant pot is the most suitable appliance for you. This book deals with everything you need to know about instant pot as a beginner and provides you over 90 mouth-watering easy-to-prepare 5-ingredient or less Instant Pot recipes.

Everybody wants to enjoy a hygienic and delicious home-cooked meal to ensure the physical health and inner happiness. If you are considering following any diet plan to lose weight, or you want to quit junk food and take-out options; but lack time to prepare the home-cooked meal for yourself and for your whole family, then the instant pot can do magic for you.

Today we are living in an ever-changing society, where it is hard to find a time to cook the satisfying meal that benefits our mental and physical health. As a result, indulging ourselves in junk food choices is a bad option, as the unhealthy food is the topmost cause of all illnesses.

Instant pot provides you with a very effective and fast way of cooking a meal that required less time, efforts, and fuel. It is a unique hand free cooking experience. If you are still confused about the effectiveness of this magical device, then let yourself know about it much deeper by reading this book.

This book is your most valuable Instant Pot guide. Meantime all recipes in this book will save you too much time and money. I think you will like all of them!

PART 1: ESSENTIAL OF INSTANT POT COOKING

CHAPTER 1: INSTANT POT BASICS

WHAT IS EXACTLY AN INSTANT POT?

If you never heard about this appliance, then the first question that came to the mind is what instant pot is and how it works? Well, instant pot is a single appliance with multiple purposes. You can find the wide variety of this appliance in a market and online shopping stores. It is a very smart device that saves you money, fuel, and time. It is currently used by millions of people around the world. The food prepared inside the instant pot is not only well texture but yummy and delicious.

It is a magical appliance that makes cooking easy. It is the single appliance with several functions. It can be a pressure cooker, steamer, warming pot, and the rice cooker. Usually, it speeds up the cooking process 10 times more than traditional methods. It is an energy efficient appliance as it uses 70-80 percent of less energy. We can say that it is a budget-oriented appliance that anyone can buy to make the life easier.

HOW DOES AN INSTANT POT WORK?

The mechanism of instant pot is simple. First, you need to compile the list of ingredients for the recipe you are preparing. Remember not to fill the instant pot with excessive content. Once the instant pot is dumped with ingredients, lock the lid and turn on the pot and let the magic begin.

Set the timer for the meal to cook at the defined pressure. The temperature starts increasing inside the pot, which creates the steam. As the pot is locked, the steam started to build inside the pot. As there is no room for the steam to escape, the boiling point increase and the hyper steam cause the food to cook quickly.

HISTORY OF THE INSTANT POT

A French physicist named Denis Papin invented instant pot in 1679. During the Second World War, it gains popularity and become a widely used household appliance.

The Midea group manufactures the instant pot in recent years. In 2008, Robert Wang and You Quin introduced a new design for the instant pot. They proposed the new design for instant pot in 2010, namely instant pot pressure cooker.

Their model introduces different features like a pressure cooker, slow cooker, rice cooker, yogurt maker, sauté pan, steamer, and food warmer. The model remains underdeveloped for 18 months before final release.

In 2015, the instant pot was recalled with the selling of 1140 units. Because of its peak trends, the instant pot gains the high reputation, as more than thousands of posts were made on social media like Facebook, Twitter, and the Instagram. The internet community was created by the name of pothead abbreviation for instant pot users. Till 2017, the instant pot was one of the top 5 best-selling brands on Amazon.

No doubt an instant pot is an amazing appliance. Here are some of the pros and cons of the pot.

CHAPTER 2: PROS AND CONS OF INSTANT POT COOKING

PROS OF INSTANT POT

- It can save a lot of our time as it is a pressure cooker running on steroids.
- It can steam and sauté the ingredients.
- You can prepare some of the finest meals without babysitting the appliance.
- Frozen meals are cooked to perfection in the instant pot.
- Within a reasonable amount of time, you can prepare froze chicken, pork, right at your dinner table.
- It is an appliance with the versatility as it can cook yogurt, boiled eggs, and desserts as well.
- It can prepare some finest and delicious one pot meals. It is a great tool to help you out in menu planning.

CONS OF INSTANT POT

Despite being at its peak trends, here are some back draws of the instant pot.
- It does not prepare the complete meal in 10 minutes; you need to wait for 20 minutes. So, it's not a super fast appliance for cooking. The heat and pressure depend upon the content you are putting into the device.
- As it is an electronic appliance, therefore many technical issues occur like venting and sealing issues. Sometimes delayed timer issues appear. Sometimes the liquids blast out of the steam enough to hit the ceiling.
- The dairy products transform into curd inside the instant pot.

CHAPTER 3: WHERE AND HOW TO BUY A GOOD INSTANT POT?

Instant pot is one of the effective appliances, which make the daily cooking process easy for you. Choosing and buying an instant pot for oneself depends upon personal preferences and needs. Today, many companies compete to provide some best quality instant pot at reasonable prices.

There are several models and brands available in the market that carter the daily needs of the buyer according to budget. The buying decision is made according to price, size, and functions of an instant pot. If you are thinking to buy one for yourself to make the cooking process much enjoyable and healthy, then you can visit your local instant pot stores or online websites. Reportedly, most of the people buy the instant pot from www.amazon.com.
If you find it difficult to choose from the wide variety of instant pot, below is the list that may help you in choosing one.

1. LUX 6-IN1 MODEL

This model of instant pot doesn't come with variable temperatures and is not suitable to make yogurt. You cannot cook food at low pressure in this model. The sterilizer option is not available. The self-closing valve option is not available as well. It provides high-pressure cooking and comes with sauté button, keeps warm button, steam, slow cook button, and rice maker option. Its body is made of stainless steel.

2. DUO 7-IN-1 MODEL

This model of instant pot also doesn't come with variable temperature and sterilizer. It can make yogurt and cook food at low pressure as well as high. It has buttons like; keep warm, steam button, slow cook button, and the rice-maker. The lid rests on the handle. The body is stainless steel. The self-closing valve option is not available.

3. SMART MILLION-IN-1 MODEL

It offers variable temperate, but no sterilizer. It offers yogurt making and cooks food at low pressure as well as high. It has the keep warm button, steam button, slow cook button, and rice cooking option. The lid rests on the handle. The body is stainless steel. The self-closing valve option is not available.

4. DUO PLUS 9-IN-1 MODEL

It has options like Sterilizer, but no variable temperature is available. It offers yogurt making. It cooks food at low pressure as well as high pressure. It has a sauté button, keeps warm button, slow cook button, steam button, and rice maker button. Its body is made of stainless steel. The lid rests on the handle. The self-closing valve option is not available.

5. ULTRA 10-IN-1 MODEL

This model provides all the functions, which no other model can provide. It has options like:

- Variable temperature
- Sterilizer
- Makes yogurt option
- Cook food at low pressure
- Cook food at high pressure
- Sauté button
- Keep warm button
- Slow cook button
- Steam button
- Rice maker option

Its lid rest on the handle and self-closing valve option are available as well.

CHAPTER 4: A DEEPER LOOKING INSIDE OF INSTANT POT

THE BUTTONS AND FUNCTIONS OF INSTANT POT

If you make a decision to buy an instant pot for a magical cooking experience, then it's crucial to know how it operates. Let us look at the buttons and its function.

- The button with the mark + and – is used to set the cooking time.
- The pressure button changes the pressure while cooking from low to high.
- The manual button is used to adjust the setting that is related to cooking from high to low pressure.
- The cancel button cancels the current function.
- The adjust button set the temperature for cooking food.
- The sauté button is used to sauté the ingredients.
- The slow cook button is used for slow cooking.
- To steam the content, you need to press the steam button.

There are two steam release options available in instant pot. One is quick release, which happens when you release the handle by manually turning it from sealing to vent. The other option is natural release; the natural release is when steam escapes naturally within 10 minutes.

HOW TO MAINTAIN AN INSTANT POT?

After buying an instant pot, it's also important to maintain it for reliability, durability, and quality performance for the long-term.

- To keep the instant pot well maintained, keep it clean.
- Wash and clean the instant pot after cooking.
- Use warm water with dishwashing soap to clean the instant pot inner pot.
- Keep checking instant pot parts, whether any of it needs repair or replacement.
- Sealing ring should be monitored for replacement as well.

COOKING TIME FOR VARIOUS FOOD

Different food items required different cooking time when using an instant pot. This portion of the chapter cover cooking time for most of the food items in order to help you prepare the finest and delicious meal on daily bases.

Food List Along With the Cooking Time
- Beef, Mutton, Red Meat 25-40 Minutes
- Chicken 10-15 Minutes
- Turkey Meat 20 Minutes
- Fish and Sea Food 3-6 Minutes
- Organic Egg 2-4 Minutes
- Spaghetti/ Pasta 5 Minutes
- Pork Meat 55 Minutes
- White Rice 15 Minutes
- Grains 25-30 Minutes
- Lentils 10-30 Minutes
- Brown Rice 25 Minutes
- Potatoes 10 Minutes
- Soybeans 2-30 Minutes

CHAPTER 5: TIPS AND CAUTIONS OF INSTANT POT COOKING

While you're cooking food in an instant pot, don't leave the appliance alone for too long. Use trivets or the cooking racks to keep the food out of a liquid.

- Instant Pot is not suitable for frying.
- Use the sauté button to perform sautéing.
- Never open the pot while it is in pressure mode.
- Change the sealing ring if loosen or cracked.
- Change the inner pot and lids of the instant pot if needed.
- Always cook the content with some amount of liquid to keep the pressure maintained.
- Replace the sealing ring every 6-8 months.
- Keep the sealing perfectly attached before cooking the content inside the instant pot.
- Never overflow the pot with the contents.
- Once done with the cooking release the steam by using quick or natural release method, then open the pot.
- Keep the appliance dry.
- Keep it upward.
- Don't step on the appliance.

SOME GOOD INSTANT POT TERMINOLOGIES FOR BEGINNERS

If you buy an instant pot, then you need to know about some of its terminologies that are widely used.

- PC: It stands for a pressure cooker.
- Nut bag is a term used for mesh bag.
- Pothead: this term is used for instant pot user.
- IP: It stands for the instant pot.
- QR: It stands for quick release steam.
- HP: It stands for high pressure.
- NR: It stands for natural release steam.

• EPC: EPC stands for an electric pressure cooker.
• The term PIP is used when the content is first placed in a heatproof bowl and then place inside pot vessel.
• Sling: This term is used for foil strip made of aluminum.

CHAPTER 6: FAQS ABOUT INSTANT POT

Q. Which instant pot should you buy?
A. It depends upon your personal need. If you want to feed a family of 4; then 6 quarter instant pot is a good option.

Q. Where you can buy an instant pot?
A. You can easily buy an instant pot from your local instant pot store or online stores.

Q. Can you make yogurt in an instant pot?
A. It depends on the model of the instant pot, as some of its models don't provide this facility.

Q. Is instant pot same as pressure cooker?
A. Yes, it is a multifunctional cooker and has extra functions as compared to traditional cooker.

Q. Is it called instapot?
A. Yes, many users use this term as well, but the correct term is instant pot.

Q. Is cooking meal in instant pot easy?
A. Yes, it is 10 times much easier than the traditional method.

Q. Is instant pot safe appliance to use?
A. The certified proven safety mechanisms make it one of the safest devices to use.

Q. What is the working pressure range of instant pot?
A. The pressure range is from 10.15 to 11.6 psi.

Q. Is instant pot used for frying?
A. No, it's not.

Q. Can Instant Pot be used for Pressure Canning?
A. Well, the tests are not being done for pressure canning, so it's not been recommended by USDA.

Part 2: Quick 5-Ingredient or Less Instant Pot Recipes

Chapter 7: Delicious Meat Recipes

1. Barbecue Ribs

Serves: 4
Preparation time: 30 minutes
Ingredients:
1 rack baby back ribs
4 tablespoons barbecue rub
1 cup apple juice
1 cup vegetable broth
2 cups barbecue sauce

Preparation:
1) Discard the membrane from the ribs.
2) Coat the ribs with the barbecue rub.
3) Put the ribs inside the Instant Pot.
4) Pour in the apple juice and vegetable broth.
5) Seal the pot, and set to manual mode.
6) Cook for 20 minutes.
7) Release the pressure naturally.
8) Take the ribs out of the pot.
9) Preheat the oven to 350 degrees F.
10) Place the ribs on a baking sheet.
11) Drizzle with the barbecue sauce.
12) Broil for 5-8 minutes.
13) Serve while warm.

Serving Suggestion: Top with chopped green onion.

Tip: To double the servings, double the amount of barbecue sauce and meat rub but retain the same amount of vegetable broth and apple juice.

2. SALISBURY STEAK

Serves: 5-7
Preparation time: 20 minutes
Ingredients:
1 pack gravy powder
8 oz. mushrooms
1/2 teaspoon garlic powder
2 lb. ground beef
1/2 cup onion, chopped

Preparation:
1) Pour 1 1/2 cups of water into a pot over medium heat.
2) Bring to a boil.
3) Transfer the water to the Instant Pot.
4) Add the gravy powder and mix.
5) Add the mushrooms.
6) Sprinkle the garlic powder all over the ground beef.
7) Add the chopped onions.
8) Mix well.
9) Make 5-7 patties from the seasoned ground beef.
10) Place a steamer basket inside the Instant Pot.
11) Put the beef patties on top of the steamer basket.
12) Cover the pot.
13) Set to manual mode.
14) Cook for 6 minutes.
15) Release the pressure naturally.
16) Pour the mushroom gravy over the beef patties before serving.

Serving Suggestion: Serve this dish with green salad or mashed potatoes.

Tip: You can also add 1/4 cup chopped parsley to the beef patty mixture.

3. Meatball Spaghetti

Serves: 4
Preparation time: 30 minutes
Ingredients:
1 lb. frozen meatballs
8 oz. spaghetti noodles (uncooked)
24 oz. spaghetti sauce
1 tablespoon extra-virgin olive oil
Parmesan cheese

Preparation:
1) Place the meatballs in the Instant Pot.
2) Break the noodles in half.
3) Place the noodles on top of the meatballs.
4) Pour the olive oil, spaghetti sauce and 3 cups of water over the noodles.
5) Give it a good mix.
6) Seal the pot.
7) Set it to manual mode, and cook at high pressure for 10 minutes.
8) Do a quick pressure release.
9) Sprinkle with the Parmesan cheese before serving.

Serving Suggestion: Garnish with chopped fresh basil.

Tip: You can also make your own meatballs by mixing 1 lb. ground beef with salt, pepper and chopped onions.

4. KALUA PORK

Serves: 8
Preparation time: 1 hour and 40 minutes
Ingredients:
1 tablespoon salt
1 teaspoon smoked paprika
5 lb. pork butt meat, sliced
2 cups green cabbage, sliced

Preparation:
1) In a shallow dish, mix the salt and paprika.
2) Rub the pork with the salt mixture.
3) Put the pork inside the Instant Pot.
4) Pour in 1 cup of water.
5) Seal the pot.
6) Choose manual setting.
7) Set it to high pressure at 90 minutes.
8) Release the pressure naturally.
9) Transfer the pork to a bowl.
10) Cover with foil to keep warm.
11) Add the cabbage to the Instant Pot.
12) Stir to coat with the juices.
13) Place the lid.
14) Set it to manual and cook for 3 minutes.
15) Release the pressure naturally.
16) Serve the pork with the green cabbage.

Serving Suggestion: Serve with potato salad or rice.

Tip: It's also a good idea to marinate the pork for at least 30 minutes to let the spices seep into the meat.

5. SAUSAGE & CABBAGE

Serves: 4
Preparation time: 10 minutes
Ingredients:
3 tablespoons coconut oil
1 lb. sausage links, sliced
1/2 cup onion, chopped
2 cups green cabbage, chopped
Salt and pepper to taste
Preparation:
1) Choose the sauté mode in the Instant Pot. Pour the coconut oil.
2) Add the sausage and cook until slightly brown. Add the onion and cabbage.
3) Add 1 cup of water. Season with the salt and pepper. Cover the pot.
4) Cook at high pressure for 1 minute.
5) Release the pressure quickly.
6) Let cool before serving.
Serving Suggestion: Serve this dish with brown rice.
Tip: Add a cup of diced tomatoes instead of water for a more flavorful dish.

6. ITALIAN BEEF

Serves: 4-6
Preparation time: 1 hour and 20 minutes
Ingredients:
2 tablespoons olive oil
3 lb. beef roast
2 tablespoons garlic, minced
2 cups beef broth
12 oz. jar pepperoncini, stems removed
Preparation:
1) Set the Instant Pot to sauté function. Pour in the olive oil.
2) Brown the roast for 3-4 minutes per side.
3) Add the garlic, beef broth, pepperoncini and half of the liquid from the jar.
4) Cover the pot. Choose the stew setting. Cook for 80 minutes.
5) Release the pressure naturally. Shred the beef using 2 forks.
6) Put the shredded beef back to the pot and mix with the juices.
Serving Suggestion: Serve with hamburger buns, and your choice of cheese. Ideal options are mozzarella, cheddar and provolone.
Tip: Reduce cooking time by slicing the beef into smaller chunks.

7. RANCH PORK CHOPS

Serves: 4
Preparation time: 20 minutes
Ingredients:
2 lb. boneless pork chops
1 oz. ranch dressing mix
12 oz. cream of chicken soup
Preparation:
1) Add all the ingredients in the Instant Pot.
2) Pour in 1 1/4 cups of water.
3) Stir to combine.
4) Lock the lid in place.
5) Cook at high pressure for 15 minutes.
6) Release the pressure naturally.
Serving Suggestion: Serve with green leafy salad.

Tip: You can also mix all the ingredients and freeze if you want to cook it the next day.

8. HAM WITH CRANBERRY SAUCE

Serves: 10
Preparation time: 60 minutes
Ingredients:
5 lb. hickory smoked ham
8 oz. cranberry sauce
10 oz. canned crushed pineapples, undrained
Preparation:
1) Place the ham in the Instant Pot.
2) Pour in the cranberry sauce and crushed pineapples.
3) Mix well.
4) Seal the pot.
5) Choose the meat setting.
6) Cook for 40 minutes.
7) Release the pressure naturally.

Tip: Include the juice from the canned pineapples for a sweeter flavor.

9. POT ROAST

Serves: 4-6
Preparation time: 1 hour and 30 minutes
Ingredients:
2 cups beef broth
2 lb. beef chuck roast
4 potatoes, quartered
4 carrots, sliced
1 tablespoon steak seasoning

Preparation:
1) Pour the beef broth into the Instant Pot.
2) Add the roast.
3) Secure the pot.
4) Set it to manual and cook at high pressure for 1 hour.
5) Do a quick pressure release.
6) Remove the lid.
7) Add the carrots and potatoes.
8) Sprinkle with the steak seasoning.
9) Mix well.
10) Cover the pot.
11) Cook at high pressure for 5 minutes.
12) Let sit for 5 minutes before releasing the pressure quickly.
13) Slice the meat and drizzle with the juices before serving with the carrots and potatoes.

Serving Suggestion: Serve with green salad.

Tip: To thicken the gravy, add a mix of cornstarch and water to the cooking liquid.

10. Lemon Pepper Pork Chops

Serves: 2
Preparation time: 25 minutes
Ingredients:
2 pork chops
2 tablespoons lemon pepper
1 tablespoon olive oil
1/4 cup apple juice

Preparation:
1) Season the pork chops with lemon pepper.
2) Set the Instant Pot to sauté.
3) Pour in the olive oil.
4) Brown the pork chops on both sides.
5) Deglaze the pot with the apple juice.
6) Scrape the brown bits with a wooden spoon.
7) Pour in the apple juice.
8) Seal the pot.
9) Set it to manual function.
10) Cook at high pressure for 10 minutes.
11) Drizzle the pork chops with cooking liquid before serving.

Serving Suggestion: Serve with any vegetable dish or green salad.

Tip: After seasoning the pork chops, let sit for a few minutes before cooking.

11. HAM & BEANS

Serves: 4
Preparation time: 40 minutes
Ingredients:
2 lb. spiral-sliced ham
3 cups pinto beans
1 onion, chopped
Salt to taste
Preparation:
1) Add all the ingredients except the salt in the Instant Pot.
2) Pour water into the pot until the ham and beans are covered.
3) Set to manual and cook at high pressure for 30 minutes.
4) Do a natural pressure release.
5) Season with the salt before serving.

Serving Suggestion: Garnish with chopped roasted almonds.
Tip: You can also season the ham with pepper if you'd like a bit of spicy flavor.

12. CHIPOTLE BEEF BRISKET

Serves: 5
Preparation time: 1 hour and 20 minutes
Ingredients:
1 tablespoon olive oil
3 1/2 lb. beef brisket, sliced
2 tablespoons chipotle powder
Salt to taste
Preparation:
1) Set the Instant Pot to saute mode. Pour in the olive oil.
2) Season the beef brisket with the chipotle powder.
3) Add the beef to the pot.
4) Cook for 2-3 minutes or until brown on both sides.
5) Add 1 cup of water to the pot. Seal the pot.
6) Select the stew option.
7) Cook for 70 minutes.
8) Release the pressure naturally.
9) Season with the salt before serving.
Serving Suggestion: Garnish with ¼ cup chopped cilantro.
Tip: Cook the beef in batches to brown evenly.

13. Sweetened Pork Tenderloin

Serves: 2
Preparation time: 30 minutes
Ingredients:
2 tablespoons olive oil
1 lb. pork tenderloin
2 apples, cored and sliced
1 cup sweetened apple juice
Salt to taste

Preparation:
1) Choose the saute setting in the Instant Pot.
2) Add the olive oil.
3) Brown the pork on both sides.
4) Transfer the pork to a plate.
5) Add the apples and apple juice in the Instant Pot.
6) Scrape the brown bits using a wooden spoon.
7) Cook the sauce until reduced to half.
8) Sprinkle the pork with salt.
9) Put it back to the Instant Pot.
10) Cover the pot.
11) Press the manual function.
12) Cook at high pressure for 20 minutes.
13) Release the pressure naturally.
14) Serve the pork tenderloin with apples.

Serving Suggestion: Sprinkle with chopped parsley for garnish.

Tip: Add brown sugar if you like it sweeter.

14. CORNED BEEF

Serves: 2-3
Preparation time: 1 hour and 30 minutes
Ingredients:
2.5 lb. corned beef
1 cup low sodium vegetable broth
2 cups carrot, sliced
2 cups cabbage, sliced

Preparation:
1) Add the corned beef and seasoning package to the Instant Pot.
2) Pour in the vegetable broth and 1 cup of water.
3) Cover the pot.
4) Select manual mode and cook at high pressure for 85 minutes.
5) Release the pressure quickly.
6) Transfer the beef to a serving platter.
7) Add the carrots and cabbage to the pot.
8) Seal the pot.
9) Cook at high pressure for 4 minutes.
10) Do a quick pressure release.
11) Stir in the veggies into the beef before serving.

Serving Suggestion: Serve with mustard or hot sauce.

Tip: You can also use other vegetables such as potatoes.

Chapter 8: Mouth-watering Poultry Recipes

1. Chicken Enchilada

Serves: 2-3
Preparation time: 20 minutes
Ingredients:
3 chicken breasts
2 cups red enchilada sauce
3 cups cheddar cheese, grated
1 cup black olives sliced

Preparation:
1) Put the chicken breasts in the Instant Pot.
2) Pour the enchilada sauce over the chicken.
3) Seal the pot.
4) Choose the poultry function, and set timer to 10 minutes.
5) Release the pressure quickly.
6) Take the chicken out, and shred using 2 forks.
7) Sprinkle with the cheese and black olives.

Serving Suggestion: You can also serve this dish with corn tortillas, sour cream and cilantro.

Tip: If your Instant Pot does not have poultry function, select manual and cook at high pressure for 15 minutes.

2. HONEY BALSAMIC CHICKEN DRUMSTICKS

Serves: 8-10
Preparation time: 20 minutes
Ingredients:
3 cloves garlic, minced
1/4 cup honey
1/2 cup balsamic vinegar
8-10 chicken drumsticks
Salt and pepper to taste

Preparation:
1) Mix the garlic, honey and balsamic vinegar.
2) Pour this mixture into the Instant Pot.
3) Season the chicken drumsticks with the salt and pepper.
4) Add the chicken to the pot.
5) Turn to coat evenly with the sauce.
6) Seal the pot.
7) Choose manual mode.
8) Cook at high pressure for 10 minutes.
9) Do a quick pressure release.
10) Press the saute button.
11) Simmer until the sauce is reduced in half.
12) Transfer the chicken on a baking pan.
13) Broil in the oven at 375 degrees F for 2 minutes per side.
14) Pour the sauce over the chicken before serving.

Serving Suggestion: Enjoy this dish with a cup of steaming rice.

Tip: It's also a good idea to marinate the chicken in the honey mixture for at least 15 minutes before cooking.

3. LEMON COCONUT CHICKEN CURRY

Serves: 6
Preparation time: 40 minutes
Ingredients:
1/4 cup lemon juice
3 cups coconut milk
1 tablespoon curry powder
4 lb. chicken breast
1/2 teaspoon salt
Preparation:
1) In a bowl, combine the lemon juice, coconut milk and curry powder.
2) Pour the mixture into the Instant Pot.
3) Place the chicken breast in the pot. Seal the pot. Choose the poultry setting.
4) Release the pressure naturally. Take the chicken out and shred using 2 forks.
5) Put back the shredded meat to the pot. Mix with the sauce before serving.

Serving Suggestion: Enjoy this dish with steamed vegetables or rice.
Tip: Freshly squeezed lemon juice is best. If the chicken is not fully cooked, you can put it back to the Instant Pot and cook at high pressure for another 5-10 minutes.

4. CHICKEN SALSA

Serves: 4-6
Preparation time: 60 minutes
Ingredients:
1 lb. chicken breast
1/2 teaspoon salt
3/4 teaspoon cumin
1/4 teaspoon oregano
1 cup salsa
Preparation:
1) Season the chicken with salt, cumin and oregano. Put the chicken in the Instant Pot.
2) Pour the salsa over the chicken. Seal the pot. Select manual setting.
3) Cook at high pressure for 20 minutes.
4) Release the pressure naturally.
5) Transfer the chicken to a plate. Shred using 2 forks.
6) Pour the sauce over the shredded chicken before serving.

Serving Suggestion: Stuff chicken salsa into a taco, or serve with green salad.
Tip: Try using a chunky salsa for more texture.

5. CHICKEN LASAGNA

Serves: 4
Preparation time: 30 minutes
Ingredients:

4 tortillas
1 cup refried beans
1 1/4 cup salsa
1 1/2 cups chicken, cooked and shredded
1 1/4 cup cheddar cheese, shredded

Preparation:

1) Grease a small baking pan with cooking spray.
2) Place 2 tortillas on the pan.
3) Spread a layer of the beans, then the salsa, chicken and cheese.
4) Repeat the layers.
5) Place a steamer basket inside the Instant Pot.
6) Pour 1 cup of water into the pot.
7) Place the baking pan on top of the steamer basket.
8) Lock the lid.
9) Set it to manual and cook at high pressure for 10 minutes.
10) Release the pressure quickly.
11) Let sit for 5-10 minutes before serving.

Serving Suggestion: Sprinkle top with fresh herbs like basil or oregano before serving.

Tip: You can also combine several types of cheese like mozzarella and ricotta.

6. CHICKEN CHILI

Serves: 6
Preparation time: 30 minutes
Ingredients:
2 lb. chicken breasts
1/4 teaspoon garlic powder
1/2 teaspoon ground cumin
16 oz. salsa verde
Salt and pepper to taste

Preparation:
1) Season the chicken breasts with the garlic powder and cumin.
2) Place it in the Instant Pot.
3) Pour the salsa verde into the chicken and turn it to coat evenly.
4) Choose the poultry setting.
5) Release the pressure quickly.
6) Shred the chicken using 2 forks.
7) Season with the salt and pepper.

Serving Suggestion: Serve chicken chilli with tacos, tortillas, burritos or quesadillas.

Tip: Keep the shredded chicken for 3 days in the refrigerator, and up to 1 month in the freezer. Just make use of an airtight food container.

7. Chicken & Beans

Serves: 4
Preparation time: 20 minutes
Ingredients:
6 cups chicken stock
2 teaspoons cumin
2 cups salsa
4 cups chicken, cooked and shredded
30 oz. canned Great Northern beans, drained
Preparation:
1) Pour the chicken stock into the Instant Pot.
2) Add the cumin, salsa and cooked chicken into the pot.
3) Secure the lid.
4) Set it to manual.
5) Cook at high pressure for 8 minutes.
6) Do a quick pressure release.
7) Stir in the beans.
8) Let sit for 5 minutes before serving.

Serving Suggestion: Serve this with a bowl of diced avocado and a cup of fresh cilantro.

Tip: If the Great Northern beans are not available, you can replace these with cannellini beans.

8. CHICKEN CONGEE

Serves: 6
Preparation time: 1 hour and 5 minutes
Ingredients:
3/4 cup Jasmine rice, rinsed and drained
1 tablespoon ginger, minced
6 chicken drumsticks
Salt to taste
1 tablespoon green onion, chopped
Preparation:
1) Add the rice, ginger and chicken into the Instant Pot. Pour in 7 cups of water.
2) Cover the pot. Select manual setting. Cook at high pressure for 30 minutes.
3) Release the pressure naturally. Open the lid. Press the sauté button.
4) Keep stirring until desired consistency is reached.
5) Season with salt and sprinkle with chopped green onion.

Serving Suggestion: Try topping the congee with fried garlic bits or roasted salted peanuts.
Tip: Instead of salt, you can also use fish sauce to season the congee.

9. TURKEY VERDE & BROWN RICE

Serves: 5
Preparation time: 30 minutes
Ingredients:
3 cups chicken broth
1 lb. turkey breast
1 1/4 cups brown rice
1/2 cup salsa verde
Salt to taste
Preparation:
1) Pour in the chicken broth to the Instant Pot.
2) Add the turkey breast, rice and salsa verde.
3) Season with the salt.
4) Close the lid.
5) Set it to manual and cook at high pressure for 18 minutes.
6) Release the pressure naturally.
7) Serve while warm.

Serving Suggestion: Serve with a cup of chopped fresh cilantro.

Tip: You can also make use of white rice (preferably Jasmine rice) for this recipe.

10. BARBECUE CHICKEN WINGS

Serves: 3-4
Preparation time: 20 minutes
Ingredients:
2 lb. chicken wings
1 tablespoon garlic powder
1/2 cup barbecue sauce
Preparation:
1) Coat the chicken wings with the garlic powder. Pour 1 cup of water into the Instant Pot.
2) Place a steamer basket inside. Close the pot. Set it to manual.
3) Cook at high pressure for 5 minutes. Release the pressure naturally.
4) Open the lid. Press sauté. Add the barbecue sauce.
5) Turn to coat the chicken evenly. Cook for 5 more minutes.

Serving Suggestion: Enjoy this with green salad or potato salad.

Tip: If you want to make your own barbecue sauce, combine honey, ketchup, brown sugar and chopped onion.

11. Mediterranean Chicken

Serves: 10
Preparation time: 1 hour and 25 minutes
Ingredients:
15-20 chicken wings
3 tablespoon coconut oil
6 tablespoons white wine
5 tablespoons tarragon
Salt and pepper to taste

Preparation:
1) Marinate the chicken wings in a mixture of coconut oil, white wine, tarragon, salt and pepper. Cover with foil.
2) Refrigerate for at least 1 hour.
3) Add 1 cup of water into the Instant Pot.
4) Place a steamer basket inside the pot.
5) Place the wrapped chicken wings on top of the steamer basket.
6) Cover the pot.
7) Press manual setting.
8) Cook at high pressure for 10 minutes.
9) Release the pressure naturally.
10) Let cool for 5 minutes before serving.

Serving Suggestion: Serve with ketchup and mayonnaise.

Tip: For a more intense flavor, add more herbs such as oregano and basil.

12. Chicken Alfredo

Serves: 2
Preparation time: 30 minutes
Ingredients:
2 chicken breasts fillets
Salt and pepper to taste
2 tablespoons olive oil, divided
3 cloves garlic, crushed and minced
1 1/2 cups heavy cream

Preparation:
1) Rub the chicken breasts with salt and pepper.
2) Press the sauté function in the Instant Pot.
3) Add half of the olive oil.
4) Sear the chicken for 4 minutes per side or until golden.
5) Take the chicken out of the pot and set aside.
6) Pour the remaining olive oil into the pot.
7) Add the garlic and cook for 1 minute.
8) Pour in the heavy cream.
9) Add a cup of water.
10) Sprinkle with salt and pepper.
11) Simmer for 2 minutes.
12) Put the chicken back to the pot.
13) Cover the pot and set it to manual.
14) Cook at high pressure for 8 minutes.
15) Release the pressure naturally.

Serving Suggestion: Garnish with fresh basil or parsley.

Tip: If you want a heavier meal, consider adding pasta to the dish.

CHAPTER 9: SIMPLE-TO-MAKE SEAFOOD RECIPES

1. ORANGE GINGER SALMON

Serves: 4
Preparation time: 1 hour and 15 minutes
Ingredients:
1 lb. salmon
Salt and pepper to taste
1 cup orange marmalade
2 teaspoons ginger, minced
1 tablespoon soy sauce

Preparation:
1) Season the salmon with the salt and pepper.
2) Combine the rest of the ingredients in a bowl.
3) Place the salmon in the marinade.
4) Cover with foil and refrigerate for 1 hour.
5) Place a steamer basket inside the Instant Pot.
6) Put the salmon on top of the rack.
7) Select manual setting.
8) Cook at low pressure for 5 minutes.
9) Release the pressure naturally.

Serving Suggestion: Sprinkle with chopped green onion before serving.

Tip: Use low sugar orange marmalade.

2. STEAMED CRABS

Serves: 4-6
Preparation time: 15 minutes
Ingredients:
3 lb. frozen crab
1 1/2 tablespoon salt, divided
1/4 cup melted butter

Preparation:
1) Pour 1 cup of water into the Instant Pot.
2) Add 1/2 tablespoon of salt to the water.
3) Sprinkle the remaining salt all over the crabs.
4) Place a steamer basket inside the pot.
5) Add the crabs on top of the basket.
6) Secure the pot.
7) Press manual function.
8) Cook at high pressure for 4 minutes.
9) Release the pressure quickly.
10) Serve the crabs with melted butter.

Serving Suggestion: Serve with pickled cucumber salad or corn on the cob.

Tip: You can also steam shrimp in your Instant Pot but you have to adjust the cooking time to 2 minutes.

3. SHRIMP GUMBO

Serves: 8
Preparation time: 15 minutes
Ingredients:
2 lb. shrimp, peeled and deveined
2 onions, diced
28 oz. diced tomatoes
1/4 cup tomato paste
3 tablespoons Cajun seasoning

Preparation:
1) Add all the ingredients in the Instant Pot.
2) Pour in 1 1/2 cups of water.
3) Mix well.
4) Cover the pot.
5) Set it to manual.
6) Cook at high pressure for 5 minutes.
7) Release the pressure quickly.
8) Uncover the pot.
9) Press saute setting.
10) Let cook until the soup has thickened.

Serving Suggestion: Top off with chopped green onion and serve with cauliflower rice.

Tip: Use bone or beef broth in place of the water to boost the flavor.

4. LEMON BUTTER SALMON

Serves: 4
Preparation time: 15 minutes
Ingredients:
3 lemons
4 salmon fillets
1 tablespoon butter
Salt and pepper to taste
1 teaspoon fresh dill weed

Preparation:
1) Squeeze juice from the 2 lemons.
2) Slice remaining lemon. Set aside.
3) Pour 3/4 cup water and lemon juice into the Instant Pot.
4) Add the steamer basket inside.
5) Brush butter on both sides of the salmon fillet.
6) Season with the salt, pepper and dill weed.
7) Place these on top of the steamer basket.
8) Arrange lemon slices on top of the salmon fillets.
9) Seal the pot. Set it to manual.
10) Cook at high pressure for 8 minutes.

Serving Suggestion: Serve with fresh green salad.

Tip: Add 2 more minutes to the cooking time if the salmon fillet is frozen.

5. SHRIMP IN SPICY TOMATO SAUCE

Serves: 4
Preparation time: 15 minutes
Ingredients:
1 lb. shrimp, peeled and deveined
2 teaspoons Old Bay seasoning
1/4 cup onion, chopped
1 1/2 cups canned diced tomatoes
1/4 teaspoon Tabasco

Preparation:
1) Sprinkle the shrimp with the Old Bay seasoning.
2) Set the Instant Pot to saute.
3) Cook the onion and shrimp until the shrimp has turned opaque.
4) Add the diced tomatoes and Tabasco.
5) Cover the pot.
6) Set it to manual.
7) Cook at high pressure for 5 minutes.

Serving Suggestion: Serve with a cup of fresh cilantro

Tip: Add more flavor by stirring in a cup of bone broth and a cup of tomato sauce. Increase amount of hot sauce to your liking.

6. Shrimp with Feta & Tomatoes

Serves: 6
Preparation time: 20 minutes
Ingredients:
2 tablespoon butter
1 tablespoon garlic, minced
1 lb. shrimp, peeled and deveined
14.5 oz. canned diced tomatoes
1 cup crumbled feta cheese

Preparation:
1) Set the Instant Pot to sauté.
2) Add the butter.
3) Wait for it to melt before adding the garlic.
4) Add the shrimp.
5) Cover the pot.
6) Turn the pot to manual.
7) Cook at low pressure for 1 minute.
8) Release the pressure quickly.
9) Stir in the diced tomatoes.
10) Press the sauté function.
11) Simmer for 2 to 3 minutes.
12) Top with the feta cheese before serving.

Serving Suggestion: Garnish with chopped parsley and sliced olives. Serve with French bread and butter.

Tip: Adjust the taste by seasoning the dish with salt and pepper or dried herbs like basil.

7. CRAB QUICHE

Serves: 4
Preparation time: 1 hour and 10 minutes
Ingredients:
4 eggs
1 cup half and half
8 oz. crab meat
1 cup Swiss cheese
Salt and pepper to taste

Preparation:
1) Beat the eggs and half and half.
2) Mix in the crab meat and Swiss cheese.
3) Season with the salt and pepper.
4) Transfer the mixture to a small round baking pan.
5) Cover with foil.
6) Add 2 cups of water into your Instant Pot.
7) Place a steamer basket inside.
8) Put the baking pan on top of the steamer basket.
9) Cover and set the pot to manual.
10) Cook at high pressure for 40 minutes.
11) Let sit for 10 minutes before releasing the pressure quickly.
12) Serve while warm.

Serving Suggestion: Serve with bread slices brushed with olive oil and sprinkled with herbs.

Tip: You can also add a cup of chopped green onion to the quiche to make it even more delicious.

8. Simplified Clam Chowder

Serves: 4-6
Preparation time: 15 minutes
Ingredients:
18 oz. canned clams, undrained
3 tablespoons butter
1 onion, diced
1 1/3 cups half and half
Salt and pepper to taste

Preparation:
1) Pour clam juice into a measuring cup.
2) Add water to make 2 cups.
3) Set aside.
4) Turn the Instant Pot to sauté.
5) Add the butter and onion.
6) Season with the salt and pepper.
7) Cook for 1 to 2 minutes.
8) Pour in the clams, clam juice and water.
9) Select the manual setting.
10) Cook at high pressure for 2 minutes.
11) Release the pressure quickly.
12) Stir in the half and half.
13) Sprinkle with a little more salt and pepper.

Serving Suggestion: Garnish with chopped fresh chives and serve with bread rolls or toasted French bread slices.

Tip: Use potato or cornstarch to thicken the soup. You can also season with fresh thyme and celery.

9. SALMON WITH GARLIC POTATOES

Serves: 4
Preparation time: 30 minutes
Ingredients:
1 lb. potatoes, sliced into quarters
4 tablespoons butter, divided
Salt and pepper to taste
4 salmon fillets
4 cloves garlic, crushed and minced

Preparation:
1) Place the potatoes inside the Instant Pot.
2) Pour in 1 cup of water.
3) Add half of the butter, salt and pepper.
4) Place a steamer basket inside the pot over the potatoes.
5) Season the salmon fillet with salt and pepper.
6) Cover the pot.
7) Set it to manual and cook at high pressure for 3 minutes.
8) Release the pressure naturally.
9) Transfer the salmon to a plate.
10) Remove the steamer basket.
11) Turn the pot to sauté.
12) Add the butter and garlic.
13) Cook for 1 to 2 minutes, stirring frequently.
14) Season with a little more salt and pepper.

Serving Suggestion: Garnish with lemon wedges.

Tip: You can also add a cup of spinach or arugula. Cook at the last part until wilted.

10. FISH CURRY

Serves: 4-6
Preparation time: 20 minutes
Ingredients:
1.5 lb. fish fillets, sliced into bite-size pieces
2 garlic cloves, crushed
3 tablespoons curry powder mix
2 cups coconut milk
Salt to taste

Preparation:
1) Spray a little cooking oil in your Instant Pot.
2) Turn it to sauté mode.
3) Add the garlic.
4) Cook for 1 minute.
5) Add the curry powder.
6) Mix, and then deglaze with the coconut milk.
7) Scrape the brown bits with wooden spoon.
8) Add the fish cubes.
9) Give it a good stir.
10) Cover the pot.
11) Set it to manual.
12) Cook at low pressure for 5 minutes.
13) Release the pressure quickly.
14) Season with the salt before serving.

Serving Suggestion: Enjoy this dish with a cup of steamed rice.

Tip: Intensify the flavor of the dish by adding curry leaves.

11. COD IN LIME & GINGER SAUCE

Serves: 4
Preparation time: 15 minutes
Ingredients:
1 lime
2 tablespoons soy sauce
1 teaspoon ginger, grated
1/4 cup brown sugar
4 cod fillets

Preparation:
1) Squeeze the lemon juice from the lime.
2) Add to a bowl.
3) Mix in the soy sauce, ginger, and brown sugar.
4) Set the Instant Pot to sauté.
5) Pour the mixture into the pot
6) Bring to a simmer.
7) Add the fish to the pot.
8) Place the lid and lock.
9) Set it to manual.
10) Cook at low pressure for 1 minute.
11) Release the pressure manually.
12) Transfer the fish to a serving platter.
13) Press the sauté function to thicken the sauce.
14) Pour over the fish before serving.

Serving Suggestion: Sprinkle chopped green onion on top before serving.

Tip: You can also use lemon juice in place of lime.

12. ASIAN SALMON

Serves: 2
Preparation time: 10 minutes
Ingredients:
1 tablespoon coconut oil
1 tablespoon brown sugar
3 tablespoons coconut aminos
1/4 teaspoon paprika
2 salmon fillets

Preparation:
1) Choose the sauté mode in the Instant Pot.
2) Add the coconut oil and brown sugar.
3) Mix and simmer until the sugar has been dissolved.
4) Add the coconut aminos and paprika.
5) Place the salmon fillets with the skin side up on top of the mixture.
6) Cover the pot.
7) Set it to manual.
8) Cook at low pressure for 2 minutes.
9) Release the pressure naturally.
10) Pour the cooking liquid over the salmon before serving.

Serving Suggestion: Sprinkle with sesame seeds and chopped scallions.

Tip: Try using a different type of fish for this recipe.

13. CHINESE STYLE STEAMED FISH

Serves: 4
Preparation time: 60 minutes
Ingredients:
3 tablespoons soy sauce
1 tablespoon black bean paste
2 tablespoons rice wine
4 white fish fillets
1 teaspoon ginger, minced

Preparation:
1) Mix the soy sauce, black bean paste and rice wine in a bowl.
2) Add the fish.
3) Marinate for 30 minutes.
4) Pour 2 cups of water into the Instant Pot.
5) Place steamer basket inside the pot.
6) Put the fish fillets on top of the steamer basket.
7) Reserve the marinade.
8) Cover the pot.
9) Cook the fish at low pressure for 2 minutes.
10) Release the pressure quickly.
11) Transfer steamed fish on a platter.
12) Remove the steamer basket.
13) Press saute function in the Instant Pot.
14) Spray the pot with oil.
15) Add the ginger. Stir fry until golden.
16) Add the marinade to the pot.
17) Simmer until the sauce has thickened.
18) Pour the sauce over the fish before serving.

Serving Suggestion: Top the fish with chopped green onion and sesame seeds.

Tip: Tilapia is one of the best white fish options for this recipe.

14. BUTTER GARLIC MUSSELS

Serves: 4
Preparation time: 30 minutes
Ingredients:
2 tablespoons butter
1 onion, chopped
4 garlic cloves, crushed minced
2 lb. mussels, cleaned
1/2 cup broth

Preparation:
1) Clean the mussels thoroughly.
2) Set the Instant Pot to saute.
3) Add the onion and cook until translucent.
4) Add the garlic.
5) Cook for 1 minute, stirring frequently.
6) Set the pot to manual.
7) Add the mussels and broth.
8) Cook at low pressure for 5 minutes.
9) Release the pressure naturally.

Serving Suggestion: Squeeze a little bit of lemon juice and garnish with chopped parsley before serving.

Tip: Be sure to remove the beards and discard any opened shells.

Chapter 10: Healthy Vegan & Vegetarian Recipes

1. Eggplant with Cilantro Paste

Serves: 3-4
Preparation time: 25 minutes
Ingredients:
1 cup fresh cilantro
2 pieces green chili
Salt to taste
15 small eggplants
1 tablespoon cumin seeds

Preparation:
1) Grind the cilantro and chili.
2) Season with the salt.
3) Cut a long slit across the eggplants.
4) Stuff it with the cilantro mixture.
5) Set the Instant Pot to saute.
6) Coat the pot with cooking spray.
7) Add the cumin seeds.
8) Cook for 1-2 minutes.
9) Add the eggplants and remaining cilantro mixture.
10) Pour in 1/2 cup of water into the pot.
11) Lock the lid in place.
12) Set it to manual.
13) Cook at low pressure for 5 minutes.
14) Release the pressure naturally.

Serving Suggestion: Serve with a cup of steamed rice.

Tip: If the eggplant is not fully cooked, press saute and let it cook for a few more minutes.

2. Spaghetti Squash in Tomato Sauce

Serves: 5-7
Preparation time: 45 minutes
Ingredients:
1 spaghetti squash
1 onion, diced
2 cloves garlic, minced
2 cups tomato sauce
Salt and pepper to taste

Preparation:
1) Poke holes all over the squash.
2) Pour a cup of water into the Instant Pot.
3) Add a steamer basket inside.
4) Place the spaghetti squash on top of the steamer basket.
5) Close the pot.
6) Set it to manual.
7) Cook at high pressure for 15 minutes.
8) Release the pressure naturally.
9) Remove the squash.
10) Let it cool for 10 minutes before shredding with a fork.
11) Press the saute function in the Instant Pot.
12) Coat with cooking spray.
13) Cook the onion and garlic for 3 minutes.
14) Add the tomato sauce.
15) Simmer for 5 minutes.
16) Season with the salt and pepper.
17) Pour the sauce over the shredded spaghetti squash before serving.

Serving Suggestion: Sprinkle chopped basil on top of the spaghetti before serving.

Tip: You can also make a cream based sauce for this dish. Simply replace tomato sauce with light all purpose cream.

3. RED LENTIL CURRY

Serves: 8
Preparation time: 15 minutes
Ingredients:

2 cups dry red lentils
3 tablespoons red curry paste
2 cups coconut milk

4 cups vegetable stock
1/4 cup fresh coriander, chopped

Preparation:

1) Add the red lentils, curry paste, coconut milk and vegetable stock into the Instant Pot.
2) Cover the pot. Turn it to manual. Cook at high pressure for 8 minutes.
3) Release the pressure naturally. Serve with the chopped coriander.

Serving Suggestion: This goes well with a cup of hot rice.

Tip: If you want your dish to be creamier, simmer it by pressing saute after pressure cooking and cook until the sauce has thickened.

4. RICE & BEANS

Serves: 5

Preparation time: 45 minutes

Ingredients:

1 1/2 cup uncooked brown rice

1 cup dry red kidney beans

3 cups vegetable stock

1 cup salsa

½ cup cilantro, chopped

Preparation:

1) Add the rice and beans to the Instant Pot.
2) Pour in the vegetable stock and 2 cups of water. Mix well.
3) Top the mixture with the salsa and cilantro.
4) Cover the pot. Put it in manual mode.
5) Cook at high pressure for 25 minutes.
6) Release the pressure naturally. Wait for 10 minutes before opening the pot.

Serving Suggestion: A serving of green salad will be suitable to this recipe.

Tip: If you see that some of the beans look a little dry, give it a good mix and let sit for another 15 minutes before serving.

5. Cilantro Lemon Rice

Serves: 4
Preparation time: 20 minutes
Ingredients:

1 cup uncooked rice, rinsed

1/2 cup cilantro, chopped

Salt t0 taste

3 tablespoons lemon juice

Preparation:
1) Add the rice to the Instant Pot. Pour in 1 cup of water. Sprinkle a little salt.
2) Stir well. Place the lid. Choose the rice setting.
3) Release the pressure naturally.
4) Mix in the chopped cilantro and lemon juice.

Serving Suggestion: Garnish with lemon wedges.

Tip: Make sure to use only freshly squeezed lemon juice for this recipe.

6. Spiced Cauliflower Florets

Serves: 4
Preparation time: 15 minutes
Ingredients:
2 teaspoons mustard seeds
1 sprig curry leaves
4 cups cauliflower florets
Salt to taste
1 tbsp. ginger-garlic paste
Preparation:
1) Choose saute mode in your Instant Pot. Coat it with cooking spray.
2) Add the mustard seeds and curry leaves.
3) Add the cauliflower florets, salt and ginger-garlic paste. Mix well.
4) Cook until the well blended. Add 1 cup of water. Cover the pot.
5) Set it to manual. Cook at high pressure for 3 minutes.   Release the pressure quickly.

Serving Suggestion: Serve with bread or rice.
Tip: You can replace mustard seeds with cumin seeds.

7. CRISPY TOFU

Serves: 4
Preparation time: 30 minutes
Ingredients:
4 tablespoons vegetable oil
14 oz. firm tofu, drained and sliced into cubes
2 tablespoons ginger garlic paste
Preparation:
1) Set the Instant Pot to saute. Add the oil. Once hot, add the tofu cubes.
2) Fry until golden. Serve with the ginger-garlic paste.
Serving Suggestion: Garnish with chopped fresh cilantro.
Tip: You can also coat the tofu cubes in turmeric or any spice powder before frying.

8. VEGAN MAC & CHEESE

Serves: 6
Preparation time: 20 minutes
Ingredients:
1 lb. elbow macaroni
Salt to taste
3 tablespoons vegan butter
12 oz. unsweetened almond milk
3 cups vegan cheese
Preparation:
1) Add the elbow macaroni to the Instant Pot.
2) Pour in 4 cups of water and add a pinch of salt.
3) Lock the lid in place. Choose manual setting.
4) Cook at high pressure for 4 minutes.
5) Release the pressure quickly. Press saute mode. Stir in the butter, milk and cheese.
6) Cook for 1-2 minutes. Serve warm.

Serving Suggestion: Sprinkle chopped almonds on top.

Tip: You can make use of cheddar cheese and evaporated milk for a vegetarian version of this recipe.

9. Spiced Bell Pepper & Potatoes

Serves: 2
Preparation time: 15 minutes
Ingredients:

4 cloves garlic, minced

1 cup potato, cubed

2 bell peppers, sliced into strips

Salt to taste

1/4 teaspoon cayenne pepper

Preparation:

1) Set the Instant Pot to saute. Coat it with cooking spray. Add the garlic and cook until golden.
2) Add the potatoes and bell peppers. Season with the salt and cayenne pepper. Mix well.
3) Add 1 tablespoon of water to the Instant Pot. Cover the pot. Set it to manual.
4) Cook at high pressure for 2 minutes. Release the pressure quickly.

Serving Suggestion: Serve with vegan yogurt and garnish with cilantro.

Tip: You can add more flavor by sprinkling with dry mango powder while sautéing.

10. Vegetable Risotto

Serves: 4
Preparation time: 25 minutes
Ingredients:
1 cup asparagus, sliced thinly
1 cup broccoli florets
1 cup snap peas
Garlic salt to taste
1 1/2 cups Arborio rice
Preparation:
1) Coat the Instant Pot with cooking spray. Press saute.
2) Add the asparagus, broccoli and snap peas. Season with the garlic salt.
3) Cook for 5-6 minutes, stirring frequently. Add the rice. Stir for 2 minutes.
4) Add 4 cups water and a little more garlic salt. Cover the pot.
5) Press manual. Cook at high pressure for 7 minutes.
6) Release the pressure quickly.

Serving Suggestion: Garnish with lemon or lime wedges, and serve with freshly squeezed lemon juice.

Tip: You can add more vegetables such as spinach, leeks, onions and carrots.

Chapter 6: 11 Tasty Soups, Stews & Broth Recipes

1. Cilantro & Lemon Soup

Serves: 4
Preparation time: 20 minutes
Ingredients:
2 cups cilantro
2 teaspoons cumin seeds
2 teaspoons ginger garlic paste
1 tablespoon lemon juice
Salt to taste
Preparation:
1) Put the cilantro, cumin seeds and ginger garlic paste in a food processor.
2) Pulse until it turns into a coarse paste. Set aside. Turn the Instant Pot to saute.
3) Coat it with cooking spray. Add the cilantro paste.
4) Pour in the water. The amount depends on your desired consistency.
5) Sprinkle with the salt. Put on the lid.
6) Turn it to manual and cook at high pressure for 8 minutes.
7) Release the pressure naturally. Stir in the lemon juice before serving.
Serving Suggestion: This is best served with a stir-fry dish.
Tip: Adjust the amount of lemon juice depending on how sour you want your soup.

2. CARNITAS SOUP

Serves: 4
Preparation time: 20 minutes
Ingredients:
5-6 cups chicken broth
1 lb. potatoes, diced
4 cups carnitas
2 cups salsa
2 teaspoons ground cumin
Preparation:
1) Add all the ingredients in the Instant Pot. Cover the pot. Set it to manual.
2) Cook at high pressure for 8 minutes. Release the pressure quickly. Serve warm.

Serving Suggestion: Top the soup with fresh arugula or sliced avocado.
Tip: Add a little salt and pepper if you like.

3. Broccoli Cheese Soup

Serves: 8
Preparation time: 15 minutes
Ingredients:
1 onion, diced
4 cups chicken broth
2 cups broccoli, chopped
12 oz. evaporated milk
8 oz. cheddar cheese, grated
Preparation:
1) Spray the Instant Pot with oil. Turn it to saute mode. Add the onion and cook for 5 minutes.
2) Add the chicken broth and broccoli.
3) If you like a little more flavor, you can season it with salt and pepper. Mix well.
4) Put the lid in place. Choose manual function. Cook at high pressure for 5 minutes.
5) Do a quick pressure release. Press saute button. Stir in the evaporated milk.
6) Add the grated cheese. Ladle into serving bowls.

Serving Suggestion: Serve with toasted bread slices.
Tip: Use a food processor to speed up the chopping of the broccoli.

4. Black Bean Soup

Serves: 4
Preparation time: 45 minutes
Ingredients:
1 onion, chopped
3 cloves garlic, crushed and minced
18 oz. chorizo
2 qt. chicken broth
1 lb. black beans, rinsed and drained
Preparation:
1) Coat the Instant Pot with cooking spray. Turn it to saute. Add the onion and garlic.
2) Saute for 5 minutes. Add the chorizo and cook for 3 minutes.
3) Pour in the chicken broth and black beans.
4) Scrape the brown bits at the bottom of the pot using a wooden spoon.
5) Cover the pot. Press the bean setting. Set it to 20 minutes.
6) Release the pressure naturally. Serve warm.
Serving Suggestion: To make the soup tastier, top it with sour cream or diced tomatoes.
Tip: You can also soak the beans overnight and then cook at high pressure for 10 minutes.

5. CHICKEN & VEGETABLE STEW

Serves: 6
Preparation time: 45 minutes
Ingredients:
1 cup onion, sliced
1 cup bell pepper, sliced
1 carrot, grated
2 lb. chicken thighs (boneless)
1/4 cup soy sauce
Preparation:
1) Add the onion, bell pepper and carrots in the Instant Pot. Put the chicken on top.
2) Pour in the soy sauce. Add 1/2 cup of water. Cover the pot. Set it to manual.
3) Cook at high pressure for 20 minutes. Release the pressure quickly.
4) Take the chicken out and shred using 2 forks.
5) Put the shredded chicken back to the soup before serving.

Serving Suggestion: Serve this soup with noodles, quinoa or rice.

Tip: You can add some herbs like tarragon or rosemary.

6. THAI ZUCCHINI SOUP

Serves: 5-6
Preparation time: 35 minutes
Ingredients:
10 cups zucchini, chopped
1 tablespoon Thai curry paste
1 tablespoon brown sugar
13.5 oz. canned coconut milk
4-5 cups chicken stock
Preparation:
1) Combine all the ingredients in the Instant Pot. Seal the pot. Set it to manual.
2) Cook at high pressure for 10 minutes.
3) Release the pressure quickly. Transfer the soup in a blender. Blend until smooth.
4) Heat it in the Instant Pot by pressing saute and letting it simmer.

Serving Suggestion: Garnish with chopped basil before serving.

Tip: Season with salt and pepper if you prefer a little more flavor.

7. BEEF STEW

Serves: 4-6
Preparation time: 45 minutes
Ingredients:
2 lb. chuck roast (fat removed), sliced into cubes
1 cup canned diced or crushed tomatoes
1 onion, chopped
1/2 cup dry red wine
1 cup beef broth
Preparation:
1) Spray a little oil in your Instant Pot. Select saute setting.
2) Brown the beef cubes in batches. Add the red wine and simmer for 5 minutes.
3) Add the rest of the ingredients. Cover the pot. Set it to manual.
4) Cook at high pressure for 25 minutes.
5) Release the pressure naturally.

Serving Suggestion: Garnish with fresh Italian parsley.

Tip: If lacking in flavor, season with salt and pepper.

8. Coconut & Tomato Soup

Serves: 4
Preparation time: 20 minutes
Ingredients:
2 cups coconut milk
1 teaspoon ginger, grated
1 onion, diced
6 tomatoes, sliced into quarters
1 garlic, minced
Preparation:
1) Combine all the ingredients in the Instant Pot. Seal the pot.
2) Choose manual mode. Cook at high pressure for 5 minutes.
3) Release the pressure naturally. Transfer the mixture to a blender.
4) Pulse until smooth. Re-heat in the Instant Pot by pressing saute.
5) Serve warm.
Serving Suggestion: Drizzle with honey or agave nectar before serving.
Tip: There's no need to reheat in the Instant Pot if the soup is still warm.

9. Butternut Bisque

Serves: 4-8
Preparation time: 15 minutes
Ingredients:
2 cups onions, chopped
6 cloves garlic, crushed and minced
2 lb. butternut squash, peeled
1/8 teaspoon chipotle powder
1 cup almond milk
Preparation:
1) Spray a little oil in the Instant Pot. Choose saute setting. Cook the onions for 5 minutes.
2) Add the rest of the ingredients except the almond milk. Cover the pot.
3) Cook at high pressure for 6 minutes. Release the pressure naturally.
4) Stir in the almond milk. Add the mixture to a blender.
5) Puree until smooth and creamy.
Serving Suggestion: Serve with toasted bread slices.
Tip: Add a pinch of paprika for more flavor.

10. Chicken Broth

Serves: 10 or more
Preparation time: 2 hours and 20 minutes
Ingredients:
4 lb. chicken meat
1 onion, chopped
2 carrots, chopped
4 cloves garlic
5 sprigs fresh rosemary**Preparation:**
1) Put all the ingredients in the Instant Pot.
2) Pour in enough water to fill the 2/3 of the pot.
3) Set the pot to soup function. Cook for 120 minutes.
4) Release the pressure quickly.
5) Discard the rosemary sprigs.
6) Season with a little salt and pepper.

Serving Suggestion: Sprinkle top with chopped fresh parsley.
Tip: This can be stored in the refrigerator for 3 to 5 days or frozen up to 3 months.

11. VEGETABLE BROTH

Serves: 10
Preparation time: 45 minutes
Ingredients:
2 onions, chopped
6 mushrooms, diced
2 bay leaves
2 carrots, diced
2 tablespoons light soy sauce
Preparation:
1) Put all the ingredients in the Instant Pot.
2) Secure the lid.
3) Cook at high pressure for 15 minutes.
4) Release the pressure naturally.
5) Strain the stock.
6) Let cool.

Tip: This can be kept in the refrigerator for up to 5 days. In the freezer, it will last for up to 3 months.

12. VEGGIE STEW

Serves: 6
Preparation time: 25 minutes
Ingredients:
1 onion, chopped
1 bell pepper, chopped
14.5 oz. canned diced tomatoes with juice
4 cups pinto beans, cooked and drained
1 1/2 cups vegetable broth
Preparation:
1) Add all the ingredients in the Instant Pot.
2) Cover the pot.
3) Choose manual mode.
4) Set it to 4 minutes.
5) Press keep warm.
6) Wait for 10 minutes before releasing the pressure.
7) Serve hot.
Serving Suggestion: Enjoy this stew with freshly baked cornbread.
Tip: You can also use canary beans in place of pinto beans.

13. ASPARAGUS & SWEET POTATO BISQUE

Serves: 6-8
Preparation time: 1 5 minutes
Ingredients:
1 onion
1 1/2 lb. asparagus
2 lb. sweet potatoes
6 cups vegetable broth
4 cups almond milk
Preparation:
1) Add the onion, asparagus and sweet potatoes in the Instant Pot.
2) Pour in the vegetable broth. Seal the pot. Set it to manual.
3) Cook at high pressure for 6 minutes. Release the pressure quickly.
4) Stir in the almond milk. Transfer the mixture to a blender.
5) Pulse until smooth. Serve warm.

Serving Suggestion: Serve with black wild rice.

Tip: Broccoli can be used in place of asparagus. Add salt and pepper to infuse more flavor to the soup.

14. BUTTERNUT STEW

Serves: 6
Preparation time: 25 minutes
Ingredients:
1 cup onion chopped
14 1/2 oz. diced tomatoes
2 cups butternut squash, sliced into cubes
2 cups kidney beans cooked, rinsed and drained
3 cups vegetable broth
Preparation:
1) Put all the ingredients in the Instant Pot.
2) Mix well.
3) Cover the pot and press manual function.
4) Set cooking time to 5 minutes.
5) Press keep warm.
6) Wait for 10 minutes before releasing the pressure quickly.
7) Serve warm.
Serving Suggestion: Top with corn kernels before serving.
Tip: Be sure to include the juice from the canned diced tomatoes.

15. CHICKEN STOCK

Serves: 10 or more
Preparation time: 1 hour and 30 minutes
Ingredients:
2 1/2 lb. chicken with bones
2 onions diced,
2 celery stalks diced
2 bay leaves
4 garlic cloves crushed

Preparation:
1) Coat the Instant Pot with cooking spray.
2) Add the chicken.
3) Cook until brown.
4) Add 1 cup of water to deglaze the pot.
5) Scrape brown bits with wooden spoon.
6) Add the rest of the ingredients.
7) Pour in 9 cups of water.
8) Cover the pot.
9) Set it to manual.
10) Cook at high pressure for 1 hour.
11) Release the pressure naturally.
12) Strain the stock before storing.

Tip: Strain the stock before storing. Refrigerate for up to 5 days. If you want it to last longer, store in the freezer. Skim off the fat from the surface before using.

CHAPTER 12: GRACEFUL APPETIZER & SIDE DISH RECIPES

1. ARTICHOKES & AVOCADO DIP

Serves: 4-6
Preparation time: 15 minutes
Ingredients:
2 whole artichokes, peeled, trimmed and sliced
1 lemon
1 ripe avocado
3 tablespoons coconut cream
1 teaspoon salt

Preparation:
1) Pour 2 cups of water into the Instant Pot.
2) Add a steamer basket inside.
3) Turn it to saute.
4) Bring water to a boil.
5) Grate the lemon peel.
6) Add the lemon zest to the water.
7) Place the artichokes on top of the steamer basket.
8) Cover the pot.
9) Select manual setting.
10) Cook at high pressure for 8 minutes.
11) Do a quick pressure release.
12) Uncover the lid.
13) Take out the artichokes and set aside.
14) In a food processor, blend the avocado, coconut cream and salt.
15) Squeeze juice from the lemon and stir into the avocado mixture.
16) Serve the artichokes with the dip.

Serving Suggestion: Serve this dish with other raw vegetables like sliced carrots and zucchini.

Tip: If you don't like to use artichokes, you can replace them with asparagus.

2. BLACK EYED PEAS & CARROTS

Serves: 4-10
Preparation time: 35 minutes
Ingredients:
1 1/2 cups dried black-eyed peas rinsed and drained
1 1/2 teaspoons smoked paprika
2 teaspoons garlic powder
1 teaspoon onion powder
2 cups carrot, sliced into rounds
Preparation:
1) Add all the ingredients in the Instant Pot. Pour in 4 cups of water. Secure the pot.
2) Set it to manual. Cook at high pressure for 25 minutes.
3) Release the pressure quickly. Let cool before serving.
Serving Suggestion: Serve with fresh collard greens.
Tip: You can also add dried herbs such as thyme and oregano.

3. Honey Garlic Chicken Wings

Serves: 2-4
Preparation time: 20 minutes
Ingredients:
Garlic salt and pepper to taste
1 1/2 lb. chicken wings
1 tablespoon honey
3 tablespoons soy sauce
1 tablespoon ginger, sliced
Preparation:
1) Rub the garlic salt and pepper all over the chicken. In a bowl, combine the honey and soy sauce. Take 2 tablespoons from the mixture and set aside.
2) Marinate the chicken in the remaining mixture for 20 minutes. Set the Instant Pot to saute.
3) Coat it with cooking spray.
4) Cook the chicken wings until brown, flipping frequently to avoid burning.
5) Take the chicken out of the pot and set aside. Add the ginger slices to the pot.
6) Cook until fragrant.
7) Deglaze the pot with by pouring ½ cup of water and the reserved mixture.
8) Put the chicken wings back to the pot. Cover the pot. Cook at high pressure for 5 minutes.
9) Release the pressure naturally. Serve warm.

Serving Suggestion: Sprinkle chicken with sesame seeds before serving.
Tip: Marinate the chicken longer for a more intense flavour but cover with foil and place inside the refrigerator.

4. Chicken Liver Pate' Spread

Serves: 8-12
Preparation time: 15 minutes
Ingredients:
1 onion, chopped
3/4 lb. chicken livers
1 bay laurel leaf
1/4 cup red wine
1 tablespoon capers
Preparation:
1) Coat your Instant Pot with cooking spray. Add the onion and cook until soft.
2) Add the chicken livers and bay leaf. Cook for 2-3 minutes. Pour in the red wine.
3) Scrape the brown bits using a wooden spoon. Cover the pot. Set it to manual.
4) Cook at high pressure for 5 minutes. Release the pressure naturally. Discard the bay leaf. Transfer the contents to a food processor. Add the capers. Pulse until smooth.

Serving Suggestion: Sprinkle with chopped fresh herbs and serve with toasted French bread slices.
Tip: You can also add anchovies to the food processor before pulsing.

5. LEMON & GARLIC ARTICHOKES

Serves: 2
Preparation time: 40 minutes
Ingredients:
2 whole artichokes, washed, tops removed and trimmed
3 lemons, sliced
2 cloves garlic, sliced
4 tablespoons olive oil
Salt and pepper to taste
Preparation:
1) Rub the trimmed parts of the artichokes with 1 lemon slice.
2) Stuff garlic slices between the artichoke leaves.
3) Pour 2 cups of water into your Instant Pot. Place a steamer basket inside.
4) Place the artichokes on top of the steamer basket.
5) Cover the pot. Choose manual setting. Cook at high pressure for 7 minutes.
6) Release the pressure quickly. Transfer to a chopping board. Slice in half.
7) Remove the fuzzy part in the center. Preheat your oven to 400 degrees F.
8) Squeeze juice from the remaining lemons. Combine with the olive oil.
9) Pour the oil mixture all over the artichokes. Season with the salt and pepper.
10) Place the artichokes on a baking pan. Roast in the oven for 25 minutes.

Serving Suggestion: Garnish with chopped parsley before serving.

Tip: Reduce the amount of lemon juice if you don't want the artichokes to taste too sour.

6. PORK DUMPLINGS

Serves: 10
Preparation time: 15 minutes
Ingredients:
1/2 lb. ground pork
1/2 cup carrot, grated
Salt and pepper to taste
1 teaspoon sesame oil
20-30 round wonton wrappers
Preparation:
1) Combine the ground pork, carrot, salt, pepper and sesame oil. Mix well.
2) Scoop a small amount of the mixture and place it in the middle of the wrapper.
3) Wrap the dumpling. Place a steamer basket inside the Instant Pot.
4) Pour in 3 cups of water. Dust the steamer basket with flour.
5) Place the dumplings on top of the steamer basket. Cover the pot. Cook at high pressure for 3 minutes. Let sit for 5 minutes before doing a quick pressure release.

Serving Suggestion: Serve with a dipping sauce of soy sauce and lemon juice.
Tip: You can also add sliced mushrooms, shrimp, chopped onion or shallots to the ground pork mixture.

7. TURKEY WINGS BRAISED IN CRANBERRY SAUCE

Serves: 4-6
Preparation time: 35 minutes
Ingredients:
8 turkey wings
Salt and pepper to taste
4 tablespoons butter
1 cup canned cranberries
1 cup orange juice
Preparation:
1) Season the turkey wings with salt and pepper. Press saute function in the Instant Pot.
2) Add the butter. Let it melt before adding the turkey wings. Brown both sides of the wings.
3) Pour the cranberries and orange juice on top of the turkey.
4) Seal the pot. Cook at high pressure for 15 minutes.
5) Release the pressure naturally. Pour sauce over the wings before serving.

Serving Suggestion: Serve with potato salad or green leafy salad.
Tip: If you're going to use prepared orange juice, choose one that's unsweetened.

8. MASHED POTATOES WITH PARSNIPS

Serves: 6
Preparation time: 20 minutes
Ingredients:
3 lb. potatoes, sliced into cubes
1 lb. parsnips, sliced into rounds
Salt and pepper to taste
4 tablespoons half and half
4 tablespoons butter
Preparation:
1) Pour 2 cups of water into the Instant Pot. Add the steamer basket inside.
2) Add the potatoes and parsnips. Cover the pot. Set it to manual.
3) Cook at high pressure for 7 minutes.
4) Release the pressure quickly. Take the potatoes and parsnips out of the pot.
5) Transfer to a large bowl. Mash the potatoes and parsnips.
6) Season with the salt and pepper.
7) Stir in the half and half and butter. Mix well.

Serving Suggestion: Garnish with chopped chives before serving.

Tip: Use a potato masher to make this appetizer faster.

9. SWEET SAVORY CORN ON THE COB

Serves: 2-4
Preparation time: 25 minutes
Ingredients:
4 ears corn on the cob
1/4 teaspoon sesame oil
1 teaspoon garlic powder
3 tablespoons soy sauce
1 tablespoon sugar
Preparation:
1) Pour 1 cup of water into the Instant Pot. Add the steamer basket inside.
2) Place the corn on top of the steamer basket. Seal the pot. Set it to manual.
3) Cook at high pressure for 2 minutes. Release the pressure quickly.
4) Preheat the oven to 450 degrees F.
5) Mix the sesame oil, garlic powder, soy sauce and sugar in a bowl.
6) Brush the sauce on the corn. Bake in the oven for 5 minutes.

Serving Suggestion: Serve with buttered vegetables.

Tip: Slice the corn cobs in half for smaller portions.

10. Buttered Mushrooms

Serves: 4
Preparation time: 35 minutes
Ingredients:
4 tablespoons butter
3 cloves garlic, crushed and minced
4 cups mushrooms, stems removed
4 sprigs oregano leaves, chopped
1 cup bone broth
Preparation:
1) Turn the Instant Pot to saute. Add the butter. Cook the garlic and mushrooms for 5 minutes.
2) Add the oregano leaves to the pot. Pour in the bone broth.
3) You may also season with salt and pepper. Seal the pot. Choose manual setting.
4) Cook at high pressure for 5 minutes.
5) Release the pressure quickly. Let cool a little before serving.

Serving Suggestion: This is an ideal side dish to steak or grilled fish.

Tip: If oregano is not available, you can use other herbs like parsley.

11. Baked Potatoes

Serves: 4
Preparation time: 15 minutes
Ingredients:
2 lb. potatoes, scrubbed
½ cup sour cream
½ cup cheddar cheese
1 tablespoon crispy bacon bits

Preparation:
1) Poke the potatoes with a fork. Pour 1 cup of water in the Instant Pot.
2) Place the potatoes in the pot. Secure the lid. Cook at high pressure for 10 minutes.
3) While waiting, preheat the oven to 450 degrees F.
4) Release the pressure naturally. Take out the potatoes. Set aside.
5) Slice the potatoes in half but not all the way through.
6) Spread sour cream on the top part of the potatoes. Sprinkle cheese on top.
7) Place inside the oven and bake until the cheese has melted.
8) Top with the bacon bits before serving.

Serving Suggestion: Garnish with chopped chives or herbs.
Tip: It's also a good idea to brush the potatoes first with melted butter before cooking in the Instant Pot.

Chapter 13: Flavourful Dessert & Snack Recipes

1. Black Sesame Rice Pudding

Categories:
Serves: 6
Preparation time: 15 minutes
Ingredients:
1 cup white rice, rinsed and drained
2/3 cup sugar
5 cups whole milk
2 eggs, beaten
1 tablespoon black sesame paste
Preparation:
1) In a large bowl, mix the rice, sugar, milk, and eggs. Pour the mixture into the Instant Pot.
2) Seal the pot. Set it to manual. Cook at high pressure for 10 minutes.
3) Release the pressure naturally.
4) Turn the Instant Pot to saute. Stir in the black sesame paste. Let cool before serving.

Serving Suggestion: This can be served either warm or cold. Top with mango slices before serving.
Tip: Add a pinch of salt to the rice mixture to even out the flavor.

2. White Chocolate Crème Brulee

Serves: 2-3
Preparation time: 30 minutes
Ingredients:
4 egg yolks
1/4 cup sugar
1 1/2 cup heavy cream
1/2 teaspoon vanilla
2 1/2 tablespoons white chocolate chips**Preparation:**
   1) Beat the egg yolks. Slowly add the sugar. Mix well. Stir in the cream and vanilla.
   2) Strain through a fish mesh. Pour the mixture into ramekins. Cover the ramekins with foil.
   3) Pour 1 cup of water into the Instant Pot. Place a steamer basket inside.
   4) Place the ramekins on top of the steamer basket. Cover the pot. Choose manual mode.
   5) Cook at high pressure for 8 minutes. Do a quick pressure release.
   6) Sprinkle with the white chocolate chips before serving.

Tip: You can also sprinkle top with chopped almonds and dark chocolate shavings.

3. SWEETENED PEACHES

Serves: 5
Preparation time: 30 minutes
Ingredients:
10 fresh peaches, sliced
1 1/2 cups sugar
2 tablespoons flour
2 tablespoons cornstarch
1 teaspoon lemon juice
Preparation:
1) Mix all the ingredients in a bowl. Pour 1/2 cup of water into the Instant Pot.
2) Set it to saute. Bring the water to a boil.
3) Add the peaches and the mixture into the pot. Cook for 3-5 minutes. Serve warm.

Serving Suggestion: Serve after main course or during snack time.
Tip: Try drizzling top of the peaches with buttermilk.

4. POACHED PEARS

Serves: 6
Preparation time: 10 minutes
Ingredients:
6 ripe pears
2 cups wine
2 cups sugar
6 cinnamon sticks
1 lemon, sliced in half
Preparation:
1) Add 3 cups of water into the Instant Pot. Mix in the wine and sugar.
2) Add the cinnamon sticks. Bring to a simmer by pressing the saute function.
3) Be sure to mix frequently until the sugar has been dissolved.
4) Rub the pears with sliced lemon. Squeeze juice into the mixture.
5) Add the pears into the pot. Coat with the syrup. Cover the pot. Choose manual mode.
6) Cook at high pressure for 3 minutes.
7) Do a quick pressure release. Let cool at little before serving.

Serving Suggestion: Include the cinnamon sticks when serving.
Tip: You can also coat the pears with chocolate syrup for a sweeter treat.

5. CINNAMON RICE PUDDING

Serves: 4
Preparation time: 10 minutes
Ingredients:
4 cups sticky rice, coked
4 cups apples, chopped
2 cups sweetened almond milk
1 tablespoon cinnamon
1/4 teaspoon ground cardamom
Preparation:
1) Add all the ingredients in the Instant Pot. Secure the lid.
2) Choose manual mode. Cook at high pressure for 5 minutes.
3) Release the pressure quickly. Serve.

Serving Suggestion: Enjoy this dish either warm or cold.

Tip: Include raisins to make the dessert tastier.

6. Vanilla & Wine Pears

Serves: 4
Preparation time: 15 minutes
Ingredients:
3 cups white wine
1 1/2 cups sugar
1 cinnamon stick, broken
6 pears, peeled
1 pod vanilla bean, split open
Preparation:
1) Pour the wine into the Instant Pot. Stir in the sugar until dissolved.
2) Add the cinnamon stick, pears and vanilla. Seal the pot. Turn it to manual.
3) Cook at high pressure for 8 minutes.
4) Release the pressure naturally.
5) Take the pears out of the pot. Transfer the pears to a serving plate.
6) Choose the saute setting.
7) Simmer the sauce until it has thickened.
8) Drizzle the sauce over the pears before serving.

Serving Suggestion: Serve with a scoop of vanilla ice cream.

Tip: You can add a little lemon juice to the wine mixture.

7. BAKED APPLES

Serves: 6
Preparation time: 25 minutes
Ingredients:
6 apples, cored
1 cup red wine
1/4 cup raisins
1 teaspoon cinnamon
1/2 cup sugar
Preparation:
1) Mix all the ingredients inside the Instant Pot. Cover the pot.
2) Set it to manual. Cook at high pressure for 10 minutes.
3) Take the apples out of the pot.
4) Simmer to thicken the sauce.
5) Drizzle the syrup over the apples before serving.

Serving Suggestion: Sprinkle with a little more sugar on top before serving.
Tip: Cook faster by slicing the apples.

8. Applesauce

Serves: 10
Preparation time: 40 minutes
Ingredients:
12 apples, cored and sliced into quarters
2 tablespoons lemon juice
Preparation:
1) Add the apples into the Instant Pot.
2) Add 1 cup of water along with the lemon juice. Cover the pot. Set it to manual.
3) Cook at high pressure for 10 minutes.
4) Release the pressure naturally.
5) Transfer the mixture to a blender.
6) Blend until smooth.
7) Chill in the refrigerator before serving.

Serving Suggestion: Serve with fresh fruits or plain crackers.
Tip: Store in sealed glass jars inside the refrigerator for up to 7 days.

9. MAPLE CAJUN TRAIL MIX

Serves: 5
Preparation time: 20 minutes
Ingredients:
5 cups mixed nuts and seeds (almonds, cashews, pecans, sunflower seeds, and so on)
3 tablespoons butter
1 tablespoons Cajun seasoning
1/2 cup maple syrup
1 pinch salt
Preparation:
1) Press saute mode in the Instant Pot. Add the butter. Mix the nuts and seeds are well coated.
2) Add the Cajun seasoning, maple syrup and salt.
3) Add water if the mixture seems too sticky. Cover the pot. Set it to manual mode.
4) Cook at high pressure for 10 minutes.
5) Release the pressure quickly. Let cool before serving.

Serving Suggestion: Pair this snack with dried mango slices.

Tip: If you don't have Cajun seasoning, you can replace it with a mixture of cayenne, pepper, garlic powder, onion powder and paprika.

10. FRENCH TOAST

Serves: 4
Preparation time: 30 minutes
Ingredients:
2 eggs
2 tablespoons sugar
1 teaspoon ground cinnamon
1 cup whole milk
7 slices French bread, sliced into cubes
Preparation:
1) Grease a small cake pan with cooking spray.
2) In a bowl, beat the eggs, sugar, cinnamon and milk. Soak the bread cubes in the mixture.
3) Pour the bread cubes into the cake pan. Cover with foil
4) Pour 1 cup of water into the Instant Pot. Place a steamer basket inside the pot.
5) Put the cake pan on top of the steamer basket. Seal the pot. Set it to manual.
6) Cook at high pressure for 15 minutes.
7) Release the pressure quickly. Let cool for 5 minutes before serving.

Serving Suggestion: Top with butter, maple syrup, raisins or chocolate chips before serving.
Tip: Thickly sliced bread works best for this recipe.

11. Peaches & Oats

Serves: 4
Preparation time: 20 minutes
Ingredients:
3 tablespoons butter
2 tablespoons brown sugar
1/4 teaspoon ground cardamom
6 peaches, sliced in half and pitted
6 tablespoons rolled oats
Preparation:
1) Choose saute function in the Instant Pot. Melt the butter.
2) Stir in the brown sugar and cardamom. Add the peaches and stir to coat well.
3) Add 1 cup of water to the pot. Add the rolled oats. Mix well.
4) Cover the pot. Set it to manual. Cook at high pressure for 10 minutes.
5) Release the pressure quickly.
6) Uncover the pot. Stir before serving.
Serving Suggestion: Serve with Greek yogurt.
Tip: You can also make use of quick cooking oats if there are no rolled oats available.

12. Ham & Cheese

Serves: 6
Preparation time: 30 minutes
Ingredients:
8 eggs
6 oz. ham, sliced
4 oz. Swiss cheese, grated
Salt and pepper to taste
12 oz. sourdough bread, sliced into cubes
Preparation:
1) Line the Instant Pot with parchment paper.
2) Beat the eggs in a bowl. Season with the salt and pepper.
3) Add the bread cubes to the egg mixture. Add the ham and cheese.
4) Pour in the mixture to the pot. Secure the lid. Select manual setting.
5) Cook at high pressure for 5 minutes.
6) Release the pressure naturally.
Serving Suggestion: Garnish with chopped fresh chives.
Tip: For variety, you can also use bacon or ground beef, or other types of cheese.

13. BACON HOTDOG BITES

Serves: 4
Preparation time: 10 minutes
Ingredients:
2 cups hot dogs, sliced
4 slices hickory smoked bacon, sliced
1 cup cocktail sauce
1 cup grape jelly
Preparation:
1) Set the Instant Pot to saute. Cook the bacon until golden and crispy.
2) Drain the bacon grease. Add the hot dogs and bacon to the pot.
3) Add the cocktail sauce and jelly. Mix well.
4) Cover the pot. Set it to manual.
5) Cook at high pressure for 5 minutes.
6) Release the pressure quickly.
7) Transfer to a serving plate.
Serving Suggestion: Serve with mustard, hot sauce and other preferred condiments.
Tip: You can also add ham and pepperoni slices.

14. VANILLA YOGURT

Serves: 4
Preparation time: 11 hours and 25 minutes
Ingredients:
4 cups 2-percent milk
4 oz. yogurt
1/4 teaspoon vanilla
1 tablespoon sugar
Preparation:
1) Turn the Instant Pot to saute. Pour in the milk and bring to a boil. Let cool.
2) Add the yogurt, vanilla and sugar to the milk. Pour in the mixture into 4 cups.
3) Add 5 cups of water into the Instant Pot. Place a steamer basket inside the pot.
4) Put the cups on top of the steamer basket. Close the pot.
5) Press the keep warm function. Wait for 15 minutes.
6) Press cancelation. Let the pot stand covered for 10 hours.
7) Take out the yogurt.
8) Chill for at least 1 hour before serving.

Serving Suggestion: Enjoy vanilla yogurt with fresh fruit slices and cubed cheese.
Tip: Sugar can be replaced with honey.

15. POPCORN

Serves: 2
Preparation time: 15 minutes
Ingredients:
2 tablespoons organic coconut oil
1 tablespoon unsalted butter
1/2 cup corn kernels

Preparation:
1) Set the Instant Pot to saute.
2) Add the butter and coconut oil.
3) Add the corn kernels.
4) Cook for 3-5 minutes.
5) Seal the pot.
6) Cook until the popping is done.

Serving Suggestion: Coat with cheese or barbecue powder before serving.

CONCLUSION

Instant pot cooking will provide you too many benefits! Listed below are some of the potential benefits of the instant pot.

- It is a very efficient appliance that reduces the cooking time.
- It saves energy by reducing the cooking time more the 70 percent.
- It is a clean, fast, and quick way of cooking food.
- It offers a hand free cooking experience.
- It's removable parts are dishwasher safe.
- You can prepare some of the nutritious and healthy meals using the instant pot, as all the nutrients are sealed inside the food.
- The built-in buttons are easy to function and operate.
- The glass lid of the instant pot helps to monitor the content.
- It does not make the surrounding temperature to increase, as compared to traditional stove cooking.

After reading this book, now making any meal is not a problem for you. The instant pot provides users with all the ease to kick-start the cooking process. You can prepare the meal for breakfast, lunch, dinner, and desserts. So, enjoy a great cooking experience.